)

THE ATTACK ON PEARL HARBOR
America Enters World War II

THE ATTACK ON PEARL HARBOR
America Enters World War II

Tim McNeese

MORGAN REYNOLDS
Publishers, Inc.

620 South Elm Street, Suite 223
Greensboro, North Carolina 27406
http://www.morganreynolds.com

THE ATTACK ON PEARL HARBOR:
AMERICA ENTERS WORLD WAR II

Copyright © 2002 by Tim McNeese

Library of Congress Cataloging-in-Publication Data

McNeese, Tim.
    The attack on Pearl Harbor : America enters World War II / Tim McNeese.
        p. cm.
    Includes bibliographical references and index.
    Summary: Traces events leading up to and resulting from the December 7, 1941,
Japanese attack on American battleships at Pearl Harbor, which brought the United
States into World War II.
    ISBN 1-883846-78-1 (lib. bdg.)
    1. Pearl Harbor (Hawaii), Attack on, 1941--Juvenile literature. [1. Pearl Harbor
(Hawaii), Attack on, 1941. 2. World War, 1939-1945--Causes. 3. Japan--Foreign
relations--United States. 4. United States--Foreign relations--Japan.] I. Title.

D767.92 .M42 2001
940.54'26--dc21

                                                                    2001040193

Printed in the United States of America
First Edition

To Bev,
who studied the Ozarks while
I wrote this book
To Noah,
who has told me more about
U.S. military history than
I have read in books
To Summer,
who keeps my books
on her shelves.

Contents

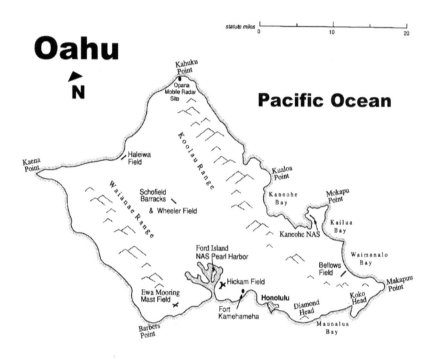

statute miles

Oahu

N

Pacific Ocean

Kahuku Point

Opana Mobile Radar Site

Koolau Range

Kaena Point

Haleiwa Field

Kualoa Point

Schofield Barracks
& Wheeler Field

Waianae Range

Kaneohe Bay

Mokapu Point

Kaneohe NAS

Kailua Bay

Ford Island
NAS Pearl Harbor

Waimanalo Bay

Bellows Field

Ewa Mooring Mast Field

Hickam Field

Honolulu

Makapuu Point

Fort Kamehameha

Diamond Head

Koko Head

Barbers Point

Maunalua Bay

The U.S. military installations at and around Pearl Harbor, situated on the Hawaiian Island of Oahu, were the target of Japan's first aggression against the United States.

Chapter One

"Asia for Asians!"

Before dawn on December 7, 1941, 200 miles north of the Hawaiian island of Oahu, 183 Japanese bomber planes lifted off from the decks of six aircraft carriers. It took less than fifteen minutes for all of the bombers to clear the decks and join the squadron of torpedo and attack planes that had already taken off.

The attack squadron's leader, Commander Mitsuo Fuchida, led the formation. Flying a high-level bomber, he listened to a weather report broadcast over KGMB, a commercial radio station based in the Hawaiian capital of Honolulu. The American radio announcer forecast clouds over the islands, particularly the mountainous areas. Fuchida was pleased: The clouds would help hide his planes until the moment of attack.

At the same time, in the waters off the coast of Oahu, U.S. Naval personnel began having curious encounters with the approaching enemy. A U.S. vessel, a mine sweeper named *Condor*, spotted a submarine periscope in waters closed to American submarines. The men on the *Condor* contacted another ship, the *Ward*, a World War I-era destroyer, and the two vessels began searching for the sub.

The gunnery officer onboard the *Ward* went below decks and awakened the ship's young skipper, Lieutenant William Outerbridge. Wearing a Japanese kimono, Lt. Outerbridge came on deck and peered out into the black sky. This was his first patrol, and he did not intend to make a mistake. He ordered all hands on deck to look for the unidentified submarine. Thirty minutes of searching yielded no visual contact. Outerbridge ordered those not on regular watch to return to their bunks.

Outerbridge chose not to report the incident to shore headquarters, even though the *Ward*'s crew continued searching the dark waters. By 5 a.m., three additional ships had joined the hunt. At 6:30, searchers aboard a fourth ship, the USS *Antares*, spotted the submarine. Three minutes later, a navy patrol plane saw the underwater craft and radioed in its location. In less than ten minutes, the *Ward* steamed into the same waters where Outerbridge himself spotted the sub less than a hundred yards away, headed in the direction of Pearl Harbor. The lieutenant gave the order and deck gunners began firing at the unauthorized submarine.

The blast of shipboard guns tore through the dawn of an otherwise quiet Sunday morning on Oahu. The *Ward*'s No. 1 gun missed its target, but the artillery men on the ship's No. 3 gun made a direct hit on the sub's conning tower, or pilot house. At that moment, a patrol plane flew in low, dropping several depth charges in the dark waters.

Soon, the Japanese midget sub bobbed to the surface, slipped onto its side, and began to sink. The *Ward*'s radio officer tapped out a coded message dictated by Outerbridge to headquarters: "WE HAVE ATTACKED, FIRED UPON AND DROPPED DEPTH CHARGES UPON SUBMARINE OPERATING IN DEFENSIVE SEA AREA."

The time was now 6:53 a.m. The message of the submarine encounter was delivered to Rear Admiral C. C. Bloch, Commandant of the 14th Naval District. After conferring with the Fleet duty officer, Captain John B. Earle, Bloch decided that the report was nothing to worry about. If a sub encounter had actually taken place, the *Ward* could take care of the matter. For the moment, he chose to take no action.

The three hours that passed between the spotting of the Japanese submarine and the first bombs falling on Pearl Harbor are three of the most critical hours in U.S. history. By 7:55 a.m., Commander Fuchida's formation of Japanese attack planes had reached their unsuspecting targets docked in the waters of Pearl Harbor. He broke radio silence at 7:49 a.m., gleeful that his planes had gone undetected until the final minutes before the attack. Radioing his fellow pilots, Fuchida repeated: "To-To-To," the first syllable of the Japanese word for "charge." Then, almost immediately, the Japanese commander repeated: "Tora! Tora! Tora!" *Tora* is Japanese for "tiger," the designated term to indicate that the Americans below were not prepared. To tell the pilots flying planes without radios of the good news, Fuchida fired a blue flare into the early morning sky. The Japanese surprise attack against American naval forces on the Hawaiian island of Oahu was underway.

In another two hours, it would all be over. This attack would become the single worst military disaster in the history of the United States Navy and would bring the United States into the most destructive war in the history of humankind.

Yet how did this attack occur without warning? How could the Japanese have planned such a well-coordinated attack for months without the Americans suspecting anything? And what motivated the Japanese to carry out such a raid, knowing fully that the result would be war with the United States?

The attack against the United States at Pearl Harbor on December 7, 1941, was not Japan's first military action of World War II. In fact, Japan had pursued a policy of aggression for over a decade.

Throughout the 1920s and 1930s, Japan struggled to adjust to the new world that emerged after World War I. While its economy was still primarily agricultural, rapid population growth (to over 80 million) had diminished the amount of land suitable for farming. Many people lived in small houses lacking running water. In a nation about the size California, only one of every six acres was farmland. This put great pressure on the Japanese government to find more space and land for its people.

There was an effort to turn away from an economy dependent on agriculture and to develop an industrial base. But the international system of trade barriers and tariffs, established by the United States and other industrial powers to protect domestic manufacturing, hindered Japan's industrial expansion.

Industrial development was also delayed by a shortage of raw materials. Many of the materials needed for manufacturing—oil, rubber, tin, iron—were not found in Japan. Japan's Pacific and Asian neighbors, however, had these materials in abundance. But these nations were often controlled by European powers. A great colonial movement over the previous half-century had brought dozens of Asian nations into the control of the British, French, and Dutch. East Indian oil went to the Dutch; Southeast Asian rubber found its way to France; and Burmese tin and bauxite (used in the production of aluminum products) sailed off to Great Britain.

Why should Japan, an Asian nation, not enjoy access to these raw materials, too? As the greatest nation in Asia, surely Japan had the right to Asian markets and raw materials. Then, as the world slipped into depression during the 1930s, it began to seem that Japan had everything to gain and little to lose if they "freed" their Pacific and Asian neighbors from European dominance. Such a policy would also give the Japanese more land to settle. The new rallying cry heard across Japan was simple and clear: "Asia for Asians!"

Leading the drive to create an Asian world dominated and controlled by the Japanese were the young men of the Imperial Army. Many were the children of landless peasants who had grown up in poverty. They knew first-hand the problems their country faced at home and abroad. These young officers set out early in the 1930s on a mission to bring new glory to their nation. Strongly anti-western in their beliefs, they were also determined to "restore honor and prestige" to their government. In their view, they spoke for the spirit and soul of the Japanese people, not the corrupt politicians.

To these young officers and many others in Japanese society, the emperor represented the ultimate voice of all the people. Although Japan had adopted some western democratic institutions, such as a legislature and an executive branch of government dominated by powerful administrators, ultimate power still rested with the emperor. Emperor Hirohito, who had been enthroned in 1928, held the power to enter into treaties, declare war, and command the military. Most Japanese, and particularly the more nationalistic military officers, viewed Hirohito as the spiritual embodiment of the will of the Japanese people.

In reality, Emperor Hirohito knew he had limited power over the strong-willed military. The army, in particular, chaffed at interference from civilian leaders. Although they pledged total loyalty to Hirohito's rule, he could never be certain that the loyalty was not without conditions. He knew the idea that Japan's destiny was to control Asia had gained such a hold over the minds of many Japanese that for anyone, even himself, to attempt to thwart this destiny was to put one's rule and maybe one's life at risk.

In short, Japan had managed to veil what in many

Emperor Hirohito came to power in Japan in 1928.
(Courtesy of the Library of Congress.)

ways remained a feudal social structure with the vestiges of western democratic government. But the respect for politicians who engaged in the unseemly business of compromise in order to be effective sunk as the army promised military glory. Emperor Hirohito had to navigate between these two forces.

Most of the civilian population admired the army and believed no other power in Japan could solve the nation's problems. During the years following World War I, when Japan soon found itself deep in economic depression, the military remained a center of power and prestige. The civilian government continued to pour huge amounts of money into its military, while every other part of the economy struggled. Not supporting the military could put a politician at risk of political and physical attack.

In the fall of 1931, the Imperial Army moved boldly. Japanese forces occupied the Chinese province of Manchuria, a region of nearly one half-million square miles, located on the Asian mainland. The move shocked leaders around the world, including Japanese politicians, who had not authorized or even been consulted about the attack. When the civilian government attempted to rein in the military, it was ignored. Those who protested or condemned the military's actions were soon targeted for assassination by Imperial Army officers. When Prime Minister Tsuyoshi Inukai spoke out against the Manchurian invasion, nine military officers invaded his home (after first removing their shoes in the Japanese custom) and unloaded their pistols into the seventy-five-year-old leader's body. At their trial, the officers made speeches about returning honor to their country and, with the support of the people behind them, they received minor sentences.

By 1936, the Japanese military controlled the civilian government. Few politicians dared speak out against the Imperial Army. The next year they attacked the Chinese cities of Peking and Shanghai by sending aircraft to bomb civilian targets. As the Chinese resistance dissolved, the Japanese sent in land forces to occupy the mainland cities. In the city of Nanking, Japanese troops killed 20,000 Chinese men by mowing them down under machine gun fire, dousing them with gasoline, and setting them on fire. Some were used for bayonet practice. An additional 20,000 women and young girls were brutally assaulted and murdered. The "Rape of Nanking" gave the Japanese military additional honor at home, while their actions appalled the world at large.

In the United States, President Franklin Delano Roosevelt was outraged by the Japanese attacks in China. He decided to recommit American support to the Chinese. In the fall of 1937, the president gave a speech condemning the island nation's aggression. In response, Yosuke Matsuoka, who was soon to be appointed foreign minister, reminded Roosevelt that American expansion had been at the expense of the Native Americans.

Other than protest, there was little President Roosevelt could do. During the 1930s, the vast majority of Americans were opposed to involvement in international events. After World War I, a wave of isolationism had swept over America. As the storm clouds gathered over China, Eu-

Japanese Prime Minister Yosuke Matsuoka (center) convenes with Adolf Hitler (right) aided by an interpreter (on left). *(Courtesy of the Library of Congress.)*

ropean nations were also becoming aggressive. Right-wing governments had been established in Germany and Italy. Italian Fascists ordered a military invasion against African Ethiopia, while Nazi troops occupied the French-controlled Rhineland. Such moves might have given Americans some concern, but they were resolved not to get involved. In fact, in 1935 the U.S. Congress passed a Neutrality Act, which banned the sale of weapons to any warring nation. A second act, the Neutrality Act of 1937, allowed the government to sell munitions only to nations able to pay cash. These acts eliminated the possibility of helping the Chinese, who had no money to buy weapons.

Despite public opinion, Roosevelt continued his efforts to prepare for the possibility of war. He requested and received from Congress additional funding to develop a "two-ocean navy," one in the Pacific and the other in the Atlantic. The president looked for other ways to hamper the Japanese war effort in China. He invited American businesses to stop selling certain items to Japan that might help the military, including weapons and airplanes. Although the president's call for an arms embargo against Japan was voluntary, many American companies cooperated.

Still concerned with Japanese aggression in 1939, as well as the outbreak of war in Europe, the president made another bold move designed to meet the challenge of Japanese invasion in Asia. In October, he ordered the U.S. Pacific Fleet to be moved from its California headquarters in San Diego to the Hawaiian Islands, which was then a U.S. territory. A naturally protected bay on the island of Oahu, known as Pearl Harbor, was established as the fleet's home.

Roosevelt's actions angered the Japanese and con-

President Franklin Delano Roosevelt took defensive action against the Axis Powers at the start of World War II.
(Courtesy of the Library of Congress.)

vinced them that the U.S. would stop at nothing to thwart them in what they claimed as their destiny to rule Asia. But nothing Roosevelt did stopped the Japanese Imperial Army's policies of aggression. By early 1940, the Japanese military leaders began speaking of "the Greater East Asia Co-Prosperity Sphere." The Japanese dream of expansion and domination had grown throughout the 1930s. Now the dream included bringing all of Asia to its knees, even if it put Japan on a direct collision course with the United States.

Chapter Two

Dark Clouds in the Pacific

Although the United States had stepped up its military and naval efforts in the Pacific, there were no plans to go to war with Japan. Even the move of the Pacific fleet to Pearl Harbor was intended to be only temporary. Roosevelt's attention was primarily focused on the war in Europe.

Throughout the spring and early summer of 1940, the armies of the German leader, Adolf Hitler, marched with ease into Western Europe, bowling over Norway, Holland, and Belgium, subduing nearly all opposition in just a few weeks. In June, German soldiers marched into France. By July 18, the Germans occupied Paris.

President Roosevelt requested additional military funding from Congress, which responded with a seventy percent increase for the navy. Eleven new battleships, fifty new cruisers, and dozens of destroyers were to be built. This was intended to bolster America's naval power in both the Atlantic and the Pacific.

The success of the German military in Europe also

brought a change in Japanese war policy. With the governments of their mother countries under German occupation, the Asian colonies of France, the Netherlands, and even Great Britain, were tempting targets for the Japanese. (Great Britain was desperately defending itself that summer against German aerial invasion and had little resources to use defending colonial possessions.) The American ambassador to Japan, Joseph Grew, warned, "The German military machine and their brilliant successes have gone to the Japanese head like strong wine."

 Grew's words were soon confirmed. By mid-summer of 1940, a new, hard-line Japanese government was formed, led by <u>Prince Fumimaro Konoye</u>. Strong, forceful men dominated the new cabinet, particularly Minister of War, Lieutenant General Hideki Tojo, and the highly ambitious Yosuke Matsuoka, as foreign minister. Having attended college in Portland, Oregon, Matsuoka considered himself to be an expert on the United States. He did not respect America and believed its democracy to be corrupt and weak. Soon, the Konoye government was at work creating a "New Order in Greater East Asia." The plan assumed that Germany would defeat Great Britain, leaving the British colonies in Asia defenseless against Japanese aggression. Konoye himself predicted that Japan would eventually control British, French, Dutch, and Portuguese colonies throughout the Asian Pacific.

As the new Japanese government developed its military plans, the American government became more concerned. U.S. Secretary of State Cordell Hull distrusted the Konoye government. Foreign Minister Matsuoka appeared congenial on the surface, sometimes sending Hull messages encouraging peace and goodwill between their two nations. But Matsuoka also spoke publicly about his plans for Japan's future. American newspapers quoted the foreign minister predicting ultimate victory for Japan and Germany and an end to democracy everywhere. Hull was convinced the Japanese government had sinister plans for the future and would have to be stopped.

Roosevelt responded to Secretary Hull's concerns. At the end of July 1940, Roosevelt ordered restrictions on shipments of American scrap metal, lubricating oil, and aviation fuel to the Japanese. He wanted to hamper the ability of the Japanese to wage war. In August, U.S. cryptanalysts broke the Japanese diplomatic code. Named "Operation Magic," this breakthrough allowed the U.S. government to secretly intercept and decode official Japanese messages. Now Secretary of State Hull could know with certainty what the Japanese intended to do next, despite what they might say officially. He realized that the Japanese were planning to escalate the war.

Japan soon made its plans obvious. On September 27, 1940, the Japanese officially allied themselves with the Fascist governments of Germany and Italy. This alliance created the Tripartite Pact. All across Japan, the people celebrated the alliance, enthusiastic about the possibility of Japan's future as a dominant power in Asia. Japan's confidence soared, and it pursued an even more aggressive policy. With the Netherlands in German hands, the Japanese pressured Dutch officials in the East Indies to sell them more oil. The German-controlled government of France gave the Japanese the approval to land Japanese soldiers in French Indochina (modern-day Vietnam), providing them a jump-off point for invasions into southern Asia.

In an attempt to meet the challenge of Japanese expansion in China and to deter them from invading French Indochina, President Roosevelt promised the Chinese leader, Chiang Kai-shek, dozens of American aircraft and $100 million in economic support. America's arming of the Chinese angered the Japanese government, and Japan's political leaders called for talks with U.S. officials. Negotiators were sent to Washington to discuss the widening rift between the United States and Japan, but they made little progress.

Soon, the Americans took an even harder line against the Japanese. Roosevelt refused to restore oil shipments to Japan until they ended their aggression in China, removed their forces from Indochina, and dropped out of their Tripartite Pact with Germany and Italy. The Japanese would not agree to such terms. They insisted on remaining in China and demanded an end to American support of China.

Although American and Japanese negotiations achieved little success, the meetings between the two countries continued through the fall of 1940 and into the spring of 1941. During the fruitless negotiations, the Japanese military continued with its plans. By early 1941, General Tomoyuki Yamashita had developed a strategy to be put into action should talks with America fail. His plan called for an invasion of Malaysia and the seizure of its colonial capital, Singapore. It also called for an attack against the American-controlled Philippine Islands. To gain much needed oil supplies, Yamashita's plan required Japan's seizure of the oil fields in the Dutch East Indies. To seal ultimate victory against the European Allied powers, the Japanese military wanted to close the only primary land supply road to China, the Burma Road, that stretched from India to the Chinese mainland.

The plan was bold and controversial among the highest ranks of the military. Attacking the U.S.-controlled Philippines frightened some of Yamashita's colleagues, such as the Admiral of the Combined Japanese Fleet, Isoroku Yamamoto. He thought that attacking the Philippines would start a war with the United States without doing enough to weaken America's military strength. Why not start the war in a way that would make Japan's chance of ultimate victory more likely?

By early 1941, Yamamoto had developed a plan of his own. He wanted to strike at the heart of the American military before attempting to seize the Philippines, which was occupied by a small force under the command of former U.S. Army Chief of Staff General Douglas MacArthur. Yamamoto's target was the American naval and air bases at Pearl Harbor, Hawaii. He hoped to cripple the U.S. Navy.

Yamamoto did not think that Japan could defeat the United States in a long war. He had spent several years in America and had even studied briefly at Harvard University. He had been a military spokesman at the Japanese embassy in Washington, D.C., in the 1920s. Yamamoto knew that America's ability to produce and manufacture war goods and other industrial materials would eventually overwhelm his country. As late as 1940, while speaking to a group of Japanese students, Yamamoto warned: "Japan cannot beat America . . . Therefore, Japan should not fight America."

By 1940, however, Yamamoto had resigned himself to the inevitability of war with the United States. He was determined that any first attack should destroy as much U.S. military might as possible. His plan began taking shape in the spring of 1940. The idea of attacking Pearl Harbor did not originate with Yamamoto, however. As early as 1931, Japanese naval officials had considered how to launch such an offensive. Each year, throughout the 1930s, all graduates of the Japanese Naval Academy were asked the same question on their final examination: "How would you execute a surprise assault on Pearl Harbor?"

Planning the attack gave Yamamoto many anxious moments. Sometime in January 1941, he wrote to a friend about what war with the U.S. might mean for his fellow countrymen:

> Should hostilities break out between Japan and the United States, it would not be enough that we take Guam and the Philippines, nor even Hawaii and San Francisco. To make victory certain, we would have

Isoroku Yamamoto developed the plans for bombing Pearl Harbor.
(Courtesy of the Naval Historical Foundation.)

to march into Washington and dictate the terms of peace in the White House. I wonder if our politicians . . . have confidence as to the final outcome and are prepared to make the necessary sacrifices.

Yamamoto also questioned how much the Japanese politicians understood about the realities of war. He had spent his entire career serving in the Japanese military, having seen battle as a young man in the Russo-Japanese War of 1905. He lost two fingers on his left hand during the Battle of Tsushima, a great Japanese naval victory over Russia. Although pessimistic about winning a war with America, Yamamoto was a strong patriot. He loved his country and his emperor.

He made his doubts public, as well. During a conference held in September 1940 with Prime Minister Prince Konoye, Admiral Yamamoto was blunt about Japan's prospects in defeating the Allies, especially if they included the United States: "If I am told to fight regardless of the consequences, I shall run wild for the first six months or a year, but I have utterly no confidence for the second or third year. The Tripartite Pact has been concluded, and we cannot help it. Now that the situation has come to this pass, I hope you will endeavor to avoid a Japanese-American war."

His public comments of doubt brought a fierce response from the extreme Japanese military leaders, who did not tolerate the views of anyone who disagreed with their plans. Their criticism was so severe that at one point the emperor assigned Yamamoto to sea duty to keep him from being assassinated by ultra-patriotic countrymen who thought he was a traitor.

The turning point in Japanese-American relations came on July 24 when Japanese forces, in defiance of the American requests, formally occupied French Indochina. President Roosevelt was now convinced that the Japanese had no intentions of restraining their military in Asia. Two days after the Japanese invasion of French Indochina, he declared an embargo on exports to Japan. Now Japan would be unable to purchase American oil, gasoline, metal, or other supplies necessary for continuing its expansion. Great Britain soon joined the embargo. When the Dutch governor of the East Indies joined the U.S. and England, the Japanese were crippled. The Dutch had been selling the Japanese 1.8 million tons of petroleum each year. With this supply cut off, the Japanese government faced a serious challenge. In order to maintain the military's supply of gasoline and oil, civilian uses were rationed. Many Japanese citizens soon found themselves with no gas or heating oil. In the capital city of Tokyo, most of the taxicabs stopped running. Japan was in the midst of a crisis.

Japan had only enough oil and gasoline reserves to last through the end of 1941. Something had to be done—quickly. Representatives of the Konoye-led government protested the American embargo. Japanese diplomats, speaking with U.S. Ambassador Grew, demanded that the United States stop supporting China and help supply oil to Japan. In exchange, the Japanese promised to withdraw from China at some unspecified, future date.

These vague terms were unacceptable to Secretary of State Hull, but Ambassador Grew warned Hull that he should not back Japan against a wall. Grew thought that if forced to back down by the Americans, the Konoye administration would be replaced by an even more militaristic and anti-American government.

Hull and President Roosevelt, however, intended to be firm with the Japanese. They insisted that all troops be removed from China and Indochina, that Japan drop out of the Tripartite Pact with Germany and Italy, and agree to sign a nonaggression pact with their Asian neighbors. When Hull and the president learned through Operation Magic interceptions that Japan planned to strengthen its positions in Indochina and Thailand, he became convinced that the only way to avoid a war was to present the Japanese military with a show of force.

Another ominous event occurred in the fall of 1941, when Prince Konoye resigned on October 16 under pressure from the military. His inability to force the United States to back down and the political pressure caused by the dwindling domestic oil supplies had taken their toll. Succeeding him as head of the government was the fierce and fanatical General Hideki Tojo.

There seemed to be little chance of avoiding a war between Japan and the United States. The oil embargo was considered to be an act of war by the Japanese military leaders who now firmly controlled the island nation. In their minds, the only remaining question was how the war would be carried out: Would it follow the plan of General Yamashita to strike the Philippines first, or the bold attack on Pearl Harbor envisioned by Admiral Yamamoto?

Chapter Three

"Things are Automatically Going to Happen"

As the cherry trees in Washington, D.C., bloomed in the early spring of 1941, Admiral Yamamoto was working out the details of his plan to attack Pearl Harbor. (The trees had been a gift from the Japanese thanking the U.S. for helping negotiate the end of the Russo-Japanese War of 1905.) The attack would require two aircraft carrier divisions to deliver the necessary number of planes; a destroyer squadron to, as the report read, "rescue survivors of carriers sunk by enemy counterattack"; one submarine squadron "to attack the enemy fleeing in confusion after closing in on Pearl Harbor and . . . to attack [American vessels] at the entrance of Pearl Harbor so that the entrance may be blocked by sunken ships"; and "several tankers . . . for refueling at sea."

When Yamamoto first presented his plan to the Navy General Staff, it met considerable opposition. They doubted that six aircraft carriers and twenty to thirty support vessels could cross the Pacific Ocean without being detected. Yet, the most likely route to avoid detection, the North Pacific, was home to frequent winter storms. Refueling would be another problem.

Some officers fundamentally disagreed with Yamamoto's plan. They felt there was no need to raid Pearl Harbor, since it lay so far outside any possible sphere of Japanese influence. An earlier plan to attack the Americans on the Philippine Islands, located much closer to Japan, made better sense, they said. It would be easier to carry out and had a greater probability of success.

Yamamoto patiently explained the rationale for attacking Pearl Harbor: "The U.S. [Naval] Fleet is a dagger pointed at our throat. Should war be declared . . . the length and breadth of our southern operations would be exposed to serious threat on its flank." He assured his fellow officers that the entire plan would remain top secret. He argued that any technical problems would be solved. Despite his explanations, Yamamoto's toughest critics remained unconvinced.

Among Yamamoto's closest friends was Rear Admiral Takijiro Onishi, chief of staff of the Eleventh Japanese Air Fleet. He was willing to consider Yamamoto's plan. The two men first discussed the plan in late January 1941 in Yamamoto's flag cabin aboard his command vessel, the 32,000-ton battleship *Nagato*. Yamamoto explained that a Japanese fleet would sail within five or six hundred miles of Hawaii, where torpedo bombers would be launched from one or two aircraft carriers. At this distance, the carriers could then turn about and sail into safer waters, away from a possible American retaliatory air attack. The pilots of the bombers were to fly to their Pearl Harbor targets, destroy as much of the enemy as possible, then fly back to the carriers. Because the carriers would be out of range of the returning planes, the pilots were to ditch their aircraft in the ocean and be rescued by submarines and destroyers on the lookout for their return.

Admiral Onishi liked the plan in general but disliked many of the details, such as crashing the bombers in the Pacific. He thought Yamamoto's plan could be altered and improved. In early February 1941, Onishi called on Naval Commander Minoru Genda, a thirty-six-year-old officer known to be "the most brilliant airman in the Imperial Navy." Genda had graduated first in his class in the air academy and was an ace fighter pilot and flight instructor. Well known across all of Japan for commanding a unit of daredevil pilots who performed for crowds in public demonstrations (they were known as "Genda's Flying Circus"), Genda was a man of great discipline with a keen mind and a flair for bold action.

Genda met with Onishi, who presented to him Yamamoto's plan for the Pearl Harbor attack. Genda considered the plan to be daring and of brave spirit. But he wanted to make extensive alterations. For two weeks he locked himself in his quarters aboard the carrier vessel *Kaga* revising the plan. By late February he met again with Onishi. Genda's revision of Yamamoto's plan hinged on the following strategies:

1) The attack was to be a complete surprise to the enemy to maximize its effectiveness.
2) The primary objective of the attack was to be the American aircraft carriers. Without aircraft carriers, the U.S. Pacific Fleet would be crippled.
3) The second primary objective of the attack was to be the army planes located in fields across Oahu. This would keep enemy planes from following the Japanese back to their own carriers.
4) The strike force should include as many aircraft carriers as could be spared. The more carriers, the more attack planes.
5) The attack should include all types of bombing (torpedo, dive, and high-level), not just torpedo, as Yamamoto had suggested. Genda doubted the effectiveness of Japanese planes simply dropping torpedoes in Pearl Harbor's shallow waters.
6) Fighter planes could provide protection for bomber planes.
7) The attack should take place in daylight, preferably at dawn. Japanese army and navy planes did not have adequate technology to pull off a successful nighttime raid at Pearl Harbor.
8) Given the distances to be covered by the Strike Force, refueling on the high seas would be needed, requiring the inclusion of tanker ships.
9) The entire operation must be kept in complete secrecy.

Under Genda's firm hand, the attack on Pearl Harbor finally took shape. Yamamoto organized the effort, enlisting personnel, including young Japanese pilots, to fly the attack aircraft. By late summer of 1941, Yamamoto had selected a Japanese city where his pilots could practice bombing. Kagoshima was located in southern Japan and was about the size of the Hawaiian capital of Honolulu. It was especially valuable as a training ground because the topography was similar to that of the area around Pearl Harbor. Through August and September, the countryside around Kagoshima shook from the blasts of aerial bombs cratering the ground. The people complained that the constant noise caused their chickens to stop laying eggs.

Even during the evenings training for the mission did not stop. Naval personnel constructed a large three-dimensional scale model of the island of Oahu, where Pearl Harbor was located. The seven-foot square model gave the Japanese pilots an opportunity to study their approach to the naval facility and the lay of the land. In addition, pilots studied pictures of the American naval ships located at Pearl Harbor. Pilots were trained to identify American vessels from a series of silhouette cutouts.

As the fall of 1941 arrived, Yamamoto's plans were in full swing. The Japanese pilots who would attack Pearl Harbor had perfected their maneuvers. Yet the final order for the surprise attack had not been made. Officially, the United States and Japan were still involved in negotiations. But the Japanese were becoming impatient, and in November Japanese military leaders warned that, because of the weather, an attack on Pearl Harbor would

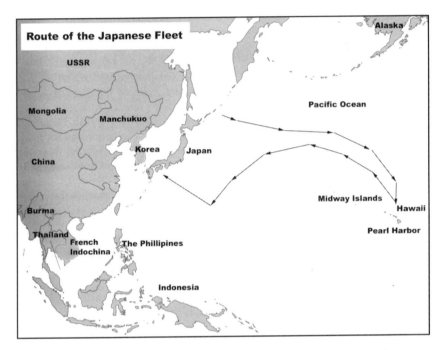

Route of the Japanese Fleet

have to take place during the first two weeks of December.

On November 5, Yamamoto outlined the scope of the Japanese plan against Pearl Harbor to his superiors. The task force of ships was to include six aircraft carriers and two battleships under the command of Admiral Chuichi Nagumo.

Two weeks after Yamamoto made his presentation, Japanese negotiators led by Ambassador Kurusu in Washington received instructions to make one final appeal to the Americans. Japan would agree to leave Indochina but would not evacuate China. In exchange, the U.S. was to cut off aid to China and to end the oil embargo. After intense discussions with President Roosevelt, Secretary of State Hull took six days before rejecting the Japanese offer. In the meantime, on November 22, Operation Magic intercepted a diplomatic cable message from Tokyo, delivered to their negotiators in Washington. It read: "THIS TIME WE MEAN IT, THAT THE DEADLINE [November 29] CANNOT BE CHANGED! AFTER THAT THINGS ARE AUTOMATICALLY GOING TO HAPPEN."

The intercepted communication sent Washington officials scrambling. They assumed that the communication referred to Japanese plans to attack the Philippines, Singapore, or the Dutch East Indies. Few thought that Hawaii would be the Japanese target. Clearly, deciphering the Japanese code did not guarantee that the message would be understood. The Japanese code referred to Secretary of State Hull as "Miss Umeko" and President Roosevelt as "Miss Kimiko." The diplomatic negotiations in Washington were called the "matrimonial question." For example, a code sentence might be translated as, "How did the matrimonial question go today?" To which the delegates would respond, "There wasn't much that was different from what Miss Umeko said yesterday."

Initially, the Japanese diplomats were not informed about plans for the attack against Pearl Harbor. They received their daily orders from Tokyo, and the cabinet did not want the negotiators to say anything that would reveal the coming attack. But when the negotiations turned tense in the latter days of November, the Japanese diplomats asked for more information from Tokyo about future plans. On November 29, the deadline set for an American proposal, Tokyo received a message from Kurusu in Washington: "Tell me what zero hour is. Otherwise I can't carry on diplomacy."

Tokyo then sent back a clear reference to their intentions to Ambassador Kurusu, and, without knowing it, into the hands of Operation Magic interceptors. The message read: "Well, then, I will tell you. Zero hour is December 8 [Tokyo date] at Pearl Harbor."

Although the Americans received the message almost as soon as did Ambassador Kurusu, it was not decoded soon enough to help prepare for the attack. Three days before the message was intercepted, on November 26, 1941, the Japanese strike force had set sail for Hawaii. The clock was now ticking, and the gears of war were set in motion.

Chapter Four

Codename: "Operation Z"

Only a U.S. agreement that Japan could continue its war in China could stop the planned December 7 attack. This was not likely, but as the Japanese fleet plowed through the waters of the Pacific toward Pearl Harbor, Ambassador Kurusu and his diplomats received orders to continue negotiations with the Americans. Kurusu was instructed to make final contact with Secretary of State Hull at one p.m. Washington time on Sunday, December 7. By then, the attack on Pearl Harbor would be underway.

Because the message intercepted by Operation Magic that outlined the attack on Pearl Harbor was not decoded until it was too late, Secretary of State Hull knew only from previous messages that the Japanese diplomats were being ordered to continue the talks while Japanese military forces were preparing to move somewhere in the Pacific. Most still thought the Japanese would attack the Philippines.

Admiral Husband E. Kimmel and U.S. Army General

Walter C. Short were warned on November 27 to expect a hostile action from Japan in the near future, but the warning did not anticipate an attack on Pearl Harbor. A message sent by the Chief of Naval Operations, Admiral Harold R. Stark, to Admiral Kimmel read:

THIS DISPATCH IS TO BE CONSIDERED A WAR WARNING X NEGOTIATIONS WITH JAPAN LOOKING TOWARD STABILIZATION OR CONDITIONS IN THE PACIFIC HAVE CEASED AND AN AGGRESSIVE MOVE BY JAPAN IS EXPECTED IN THE NEXT FEW DAYS X THE NUMBER AND EQUIPMENT OF JAPANESE TROOPS AND THE ORGANIZATION OF NAVAL TASK FORCES INDICATES AN AMPHIBIOUS EXPEDITION AGAINST EITHER THE PHILIPPINES THAI OR KRA PENINSULA OR POSSIBLY BORNEO X EXECUTE AN APPROPRIATE DEFENSIVE DEPLOYMENT PREPARATORY TO CARRYING OUT THE TASKS ASSIGNED IN WPL 46 [War Plan] X . . .

Naval authorities in Hawaii were never given direct access to the interceptions captured by Operation Magic. In fact, they were not even aware of Magic's existence. They were not informed that, as early as September, Japanese officials in Tokyo began interrogating its consulate office in Honolulu about warships at Pearl Harbor. They also did not know that by November the Imperial Consulate was transmitting naval maps of American installations to Japan on a weekly basis. In addition, on November 29, U.S. Naval Intelligence, which was supposed to monitor Japanese fleet movements, informed Admiral Kimmel that they did not know the location of the Japanese fleet.

Admiral Kimmel half-seriously asked his intelligence officers, "Do you mean to say that they could be rounding Diamond Head [a mountain located near Pearl Harbor] this minute and you wouldn't know?" Intelligence officer Lt. Commander Edward T. Layton answered: "I hope they would be sighted by now, sir." This did not satisfy or comfort Kimmel.

Admiral Kimmel considered setting sail away from Pearl Harbor but decided that his ships would be even more vulnerable on the high seas. The four aircraft carriers he needed to protect his ships at sea were not at Pearl Harbor in late November. (One was being repaired in San Diego and the other three were delivering warplanes to American bases in the Pacific.) He decided to keep his ships docked at Pearl Harbor, where they could be protected by hundreds of army planes stationed around the island of Oahu.

With hundreds of army planes at his disposal, General Short's greatest fear was land sabotage. The Hawaiian Islands were home to many Japanese Americans, and Short believed they might provide support to Japanese invaders or conspire to make a secret attack on the facilities. He decided not to locate his planes in protective concrete hangars, where he thought they would be more vulnerable to land-based sabotage. He chose to line

Admiral Husband E. Kimmel, naval commander at Pearl Harbor, thought the docked ships would be protected by American air power. *(Courtesy of the Naval Historical Foundation.)*

them up in close formations, nearly wing tip-to-wing tip on the open tarmac. This precaution made them an easy target for Japanese attack planes.

Meanwhile, "Operation Z," the codename the Japanese High Command gave to the attack on Pearl Harbor, was underway. The First Air Fleet under the command of Vice Admiral Chuichi Nagumo cut across the waters of the Pacific in grand formation. At the center of the force were the six aircraft carriers, including the Fleet's flagship, *Akagi*, plus *Hiryu*, *Kaga*, *Shokaku*, *Soryu*, and *Zuikaku*. (From the mainmast of the *Akagi* flew a forty-year-old flag from another Japanese battleship, the *Mikasa*, which had fought a battle with the Russians during the Russo-Japanese War of 1905.) The ships moved in two rows of three carriers each. The carriers held 414 combat planes to be used for defending the fleet and for attacking the Pearl Harbor installations. In addition to the carriers were two battleships, two heavy cruisers and one light cruiser, nine destroyers, and twenty-eight submarines. The submarines moved at the front of the fleet, having left their stations a few days ahead of the Japanese Strike Force. The battleships and cruisers ran parallel to the cruisers' left and right flanks, while the powerfully aggressive destroyers roamed wide. Eight tank ships used for refueling followed behind the main formation.

Following the ships' November 26 departure, the seas were calm. No winter storms hampered their movement. Some heavy clouds and fog caused low visibility, reducing the possibility of another ship spotting the Japanese ships. In case of detection by another vessel, the Japanese commanders were under strict orders on how to respond. Whether naval or merchant, no matter what nation's flag a spotted ship might be flying, the orders were the same: "Sink it. Sink anything flying any flag."

Nagumo had also ordered restrictions on communications. The ships maintained complete radio silence. By day, they communicated by signal flags; by night, they used blinkers to signal Morse Code messages. All vessels burned a high-grade fuel to keep smoke streams to a minimum. The ships' crews stored all garbage and refuse to avoid leaving a trail of debris. All emptied oil cans were crushed and stored on the ships' decks. At night, the vessels were shrouded in darkness, following orders for a complete blackout.

The path the Japanese chose ran between the American-owned Aleutian Islands and Midway Island. The route was chosen to avoid sea lanes normally used by merchant shipping. The passage near Midway was a cause of concern because it held the largest concentration of American forces in the Pacific between the Hawaiian Islands and the Philippines. However, the fleet passed north of Midway without incident.

Below decks, the pilots discussed their mission. They did not yet know where they would attack—most assumed it would be the Philippines—but they were excited about the opportunity to bring honor to their names and country. Only Admiral Nagumo and his high-ranking subordinates knew the plan's details. Onboard the *Akagi* were the scale models of the island of Oahu and

Pearl Harbor, showing in 3-D relief the mountains and valleys of the island, plus detailed renderings of the harbor, docks, land installations, and airfields. Japanese spies had collected a great deal of information for the military throughout the year. Some spying had been simple, consisting of no more than Japanese spies posing as tourists and then sending postcards of the harbor to friends in Japan. Nagumo even had intricate maps at his disposal, plus a list of the number and types of planes on the island. The detail of his information was astonishing, which even included the thickness of the hangar roofs and of battleship armor.

On Friday, November 28—two days out—the fleet ran into rough seas. Over the next few days, refueling efforts were hampered by high winds and waves. Throughout the entire weekend, the Japanese flotilla continued slowly on its eastbound course, awaiting final orders instructing them to press forward with the attack or to cancel the action and return home.

The Japanese pilots continued to go over the plan. It was a simple strategy: The attack would take place in two waves spaced an hour apart and launched from carriers located approximately 230 miles north of Oahu early on December 7, in time to arrive over their targets at eight a.m.

The first wave would include 189 aircraft, consisting of fifty high-level, or horizontal, bombers; forty torpedo bombers; fifty-four dive bombers; and forty-five swift-moving Zero fighters.

The Zeros were to lead the way and take control of the

Vice Admiral Chuichi Nagumo commanded the First Air Fleet of the Japanese navy during the attack on Pearl Harbor. *(Courtesy of the Naval Historical Foundation.)*

air over Pearl Harbor. These light, highly maneuverable planes, the pride of the Japanese navy, were ferocious fighters. Capable of speeds of up to 300 miles an hour, Zeros were able to weave and dart their way through the sky, making them difficult to shoot down. During action over China, the Zeros had proven effective against the slower Chinese planes. These small planes were fast, and they sported two machine guns and a pair of 20-mm. cannons designed to rip enemy planes to shreds.

The high-level bombers would move in behind the Zeros, showering the decks of enemy ships with bombs, while the low-flying torpedo bombers would move into position to drop their armaments, each aimed at an American battleship, in the shallow waters of the harbor. Dive bombers would focus on the airfields, including the army fields at Ford Island, located in the center of the harbor, and Hickam and Wheeler Fields.

A second bunch of horizontal and dive bombers accompanied by fighter planes would follow an hour later. This contingent consisted of fifty-four horizontal bombers, eighty-one dive-bombers, and thirty-six fighter planes. Torpedo planes were not included on the second assault because the first wave was expected to complete their mission. The second wave's objective was to neutralize the capacity of U.S. planes to launch a counterattack against the Japanese invaders. The high-level bombers were to attack airfields again, specifically at Hickam, Kaneohe, and Ford Island. The Zeros were to blast their machine guns at installations located at Wheeler Field.

When both waves of planes had destroyed most of the

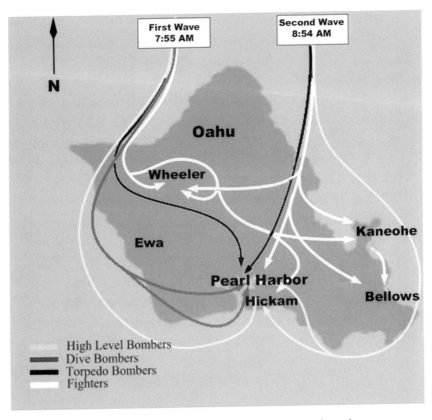

This map illustrates the Japanese First and Second Wave air attacks.

U.S. Pacific Fleet, they were to rendezvous beyond the northwestern tip of Oahu Island. Reunited, the planes would return to their launch carriers. Once landed, Naval forces were to be ready for a possible counterattack. If no attack materialized, the commanders would then consider launching another air attack.

The leader of the first wave of planes was Lieutenant Commander Mitsuo Fuchida. Handpicked by his old friend Minoru Genda (the two soldiers had met at the naval academy nearly twenty years earlier) to lead the aerial assault, thirty-nine-year old Fuchida, a longtime veteran of the Japanese navy, was known as a superior flight commander and an inspirational leader. Born in 1902, the Year of the Tiger under the Japanese calendar, Fuchida believed he possessed tiger qualities: good luck, authority, and powerful strength.

On December 1, Prime Minister Tojo met with his advisors and Emperor Hirohito. At the meeting, Tojo insisted that, because of the unwillingness of American negotiators to agree to Japan's demands, the time had come for war. Hours after the Imperial meeting, Admiral Yamamoto sent a coded message to the Pearl Harbor Strike Force: "NIITAKA-YAMA NOBORE," which translated meant, "Climb Mount Niitaka." Those receiving the message knew its meaning: "Attack as planned on December 7."

Now everyone onboard the Strike Force vessels would be informed of the fleet's mission. They were told the glory of Japan was at stake. There was great excitement among the crewmen that night as the ships of the Strike

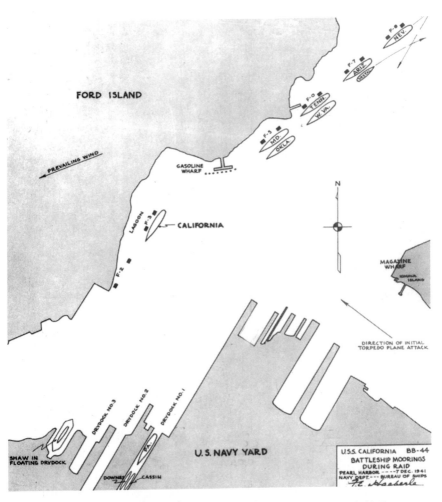

This map shows the positions and initial movements of America's ships in Battleship Row during the attack. *(Courtesy of the Naval Historical Foundation.)*

Force flotilla turned about to a southeasterly course straight for Hawaii. Suddenly, the seas through which the Strike Force passed were the calmest any of them had seen in years.

On the 3rd of December, Admiral Nagumo received verification from the Imperial Navy Headquarters in Tokyo that six U.S. battleships, the USS *Arizona, California, Maryland, Pennsylvania, Tennessee,* and *West Virginia,* were docked at Pearl Harbor. Onboard the Japanese carriers, anxious pilots sat in their planes. Bored and fidgety, some painted watercolors or wrote what they thought may be their last letters or journal entries. Bombardiers refitted and aligned their bombsights. There was little real action onboard the ships. Gunners practiced their skills by shooting down kites.

Two days later, on December 5, a Japanese spy plane flew over Pearl Harbor. That night the pilot reported his findings about the ships he had spotted to Tokyo, then it was transmitted to the Strike Force. At that moment, Pearl Harbor was home to eight U.S. battleships, three light cruisers, and sixteen destroyers. There was immediate concern that no aircraft carriers were present in the harbor, but it was too late to turn back. They could only hope that the carriers returning to Hawaii would arrive before Sunday.

Messages flowed in a steady stream from Tokyo. On December 6, a Russian ship was reported in the vicinity of the Fleet, but none was spotted. That night, an alarm went up on the *Akagi* that a light had been seen in the sky above the vessel. A call to battle stations sounded on each ship, and sailors manned their anti-aircraft guns. Only then did they realize that the "light" was a weather balloon sent up from the battleship *Kaga*.

With the attack less than twenty-four hours away, American and Japanese discussions in Washington continued. That Saturday, President Roosevelt decided to send a message to the Japanese Emperor Hirohito. In the letter, Roosevelt wrote that "a withdrawal of the Japanese forces from Indo-China would result in the assurance of peace throughout the whole of the South Pacific area." The president also expressed his belief that he and the emperor had "a sacred duty to restore traditional amity and prevent further death and destruction in the world." The message was delivered to the emperor through diplomatic channels. Foreign Minister Shigenori Togo personally handed it to the emperor that night, but both Togo and Hirohito knew the president's words could not change the course of events already set in motion.

As night fell on Saturday, December 6, assault forces moved into place. Submarines glided undetected around the island of Oahu, scouting for U.S. Naval vessels. Five of the subs came within sight of the entrance to Pearl Harbor. Once in position, each surfaced and launched a midget, two-man submarine piloted by a pair of sailors cramped inside the six foot by seventy-nine foot craft. The midget subs carried a pair of torpedoes and moved at a speed of twenty knots when fully submerged. The subs were to move into the harbor and launch their torpedoes at the battleships of their choice the next morning.

December 6, 1941, had been a typical Saturday for the

more than 50,000 American servicemen stationed at the military facilities scattered across Hawaii. Both the U.S. Army and Navy on the island of Oahu had just completed a week of intensive training, and the troops were ready for a rest. Days had passed since Admiral Kimmel and General Short had received warnings from Washington about a possible Japanese attack, and neither man had made any serious efforts to prepare.

Most of the enlisted men believed that the war would start in Europe, and Hawaii's beautiful landscape and balmy climate made it difficult for the soldiers to focus on the possibility of attack. Military duty in the Pacific was considered a leisurely post. There were the usual work details and gun drills, but service in Hawaii meant sandy beaches and nice weather year round. Regular passes were issued to give naval and army personnel opportunities to leave their bases or ship's duties.

Along the streets of nearby Honolulu, the shops were geared up for the Christmas season. Holiday lights twinkled along the streets where snow never fell. That afternoon, 24,000 islanders, including many in uniform, had attended a football game in Honolulu Stadium. The University of Hawaii Rainbows soundly defeated the visiting Willamette University Bearcats by a score of 20-6.

That evening, the bases on Oahu—Pearl Harbor, Fort Shafter, Schofield Barracks—hosted the usual parties for officers and their wives, with drinks, music, and dancing. Enlisted men jammed into Pearl Harbor's Bloch Recreation Center where uniformed musicians from docked ships competed in the fleet's "Battle of Music."

The band from the USS *Pennsylvania*, one of the harbor's eight battleships, won the competition.

Hundreds of other enlisted men prowled the streets and neighborhoods of the city looking for a livelier time. Army and naval personnel, armed with weekend passes, filled the smoky bars, crowded restaurants, and tattoo parlors along King, Hotel, and River Streets. By three a.m. the island's bars were closing. Bleary-eyed soldiers and sailors found their way back to bases, barracks, or ship's berths. By four a.m., Oahu was asleep. In the harbor, in the city, across the island, everything was quiet.

Two hundred miles to the north, at three-thirty a.m., the pilots and crews of the Japanese Strike Force were awakened. During the final minutes before taking their positions inside the planes, the pilots wrote letters to their families and cut fingernails and locks of hair to be sent to loved ones in case they did not return. As each man dressed for war, he donned a new loincloth, called *mawashi*, and a special "thousand-stitch" belt. According to tradition, each stitch represented

This Japanese pilot dons his *hachimaki* before flying into battle.

a prayer said on behalf of the wearer. Before boarding their planes, the pilots wrapped their *hachimaki* around their heads and over their helmets. *Hachimaki* were the traditional white headbands featuring a red circle symbolizing the Rising Sun of Imperial Japan. Pilots and other personnel gathered around small Shinto shrines for prayers and meditation, aware of the importance of their day's mission. At breakfast the young men ate red rice and fish, a dish usually reserved for times of celebration.

Chapter Five

The First Wave

As dawn approached on December 7, 1941, the Japanese pilots boarded the planes and revved their engines. The seas were rolling that morning, making takeoff a bit difficult, but the sky was only slightly cloudy. The planes were lined up on the decks of the various carriers: the Zeros, the high-levels, the dive bombers, and the torpedo planes. When the order was given, the planes left the decks of the carriers in rapid order, soared across the waves, and massed together at 13,000 feet. All squadrons comprising the first assault wave were airborne in fifteen minutes, breaking their record practice time. The crewmen onboard the six launch ships cheered and waved to their comrades as each took off into the early morning sky. Of the nearly 200 planes that took off under less than perfect weather conditions, only one fighter crashed into the sea. Few, if any, of the pilots in the massed squadrons had ever seen so many planes in the air at the same time.

For the next hour and a half, the largest airborne strike force in history headed south toward its target. Commander Fuchida led the force, flying most of the route to Hawaii at 9,000 feet. Fuchida's high-level bombers—called "Kates" by American naval personnel—held center stage. The dive bombers, called "Vals," flew on the left wing of the airborne force, while on the right, another group of Kates rounded out the force's formation. The Zeros—forty-three Mitsubishi Reisen fighter planes—maintained their position above Fuchida, flying nearly a mile higher than their air leader's main force.

To help keep his force of planes on an accurate course, Fuchida homed in on commercial radio station KGMB, located in Honolulu. The station had remained on the air through the early morning hours of December 7 at the request of the U.S. Navy. The radio station was also providing a homing beacon for a dozen U.S. long-range bombers, known as B-17s, due into Hawaii from California. The B-17s were scheduled to arrive at the moment the Japanese planes planned to begin bombing the military installations on Oahu.

With the planes approaching Hawaii, the midget subs began to move into position near the mouth of the harbor. At 6:30 a.m., U.S. Naval officials opened the anti-torpedo net that protected the harbor's entrance to allow the USS *Antares* to enter. At that moment, crewmen on the *Antares* spotted the conning tower of a midget sub shadowing her into the harbor. A second ship, the destroyer *Ward*, soon arrived on the scene and opened fire, hitting the Japanese sub and causing it to sink. At 6:51 a.m.,

These Japanese naval aircraft are preparing to take off for Pearl Harbor.
(Courtesy of the Naval Historical Foundation.)

Lieutenant William Outerbridge radioed in word of the encounter: "WE HAVE ATTACKED FIRED UPON AND DROPPED DEPTH CHARGES UPON SUBMARINE OPERATING IN DEFENSIVE SEA AREA."

The report made its way to several of Outerbridge's superiors but was not acted upon. Over the previous months, dozens of such sightings of enemy submarines had proven false. Few thought this sighting was any different.

Within minutes of the submarine encounter, at a radar outpost at Kahuku Point on the north side of Oahu, a giant blip appeared on Private George Elliott's five-inch radar screen. The second man in the station, Private Joseph Lockard, who was more experienced, verified the blip on the oscilloscope and encouraged Elliott to contact the Information Center. When the call went in, the pilot at the center told the two concerned privates, "Don't worry about it." He believed the large blip was the B-17s due in from California, or perhaps a squadron of planes from the USS *Enterprise*, an aircraft carrier that was sailing toward Pearl Harbor from Midway Island.

Although overcast skies had covered the approach of the attack planes, as they entered Hawaiian airspace the clouds parted, giving the Japanese pilots clear views of the docked ships.

It was 7:48 a.m. when the advance squadron of Zeros crossed within sight of Kahuku Point. Commander Fuchida took the lead position in his high-level bomber. The next question on the minds of the Japanese pilots was clear and simple: Were they approaching Pearl Harbor undetected? No American planes could be seen, and there was no anti-aircraft fire from below. Everything indicated that the goal of surprise had been achieved. At 7:49 a.m. Fuchida's radioman sent a message in Morse code back to the flotilla: "To-To-To!" This was the first syllable of the Japanese word, *Totsugeki*, or "Charge!" informing Admiral Nagumo and the Strike Fleet commanders that the attack at Pearl Harbor had begun. Four minutes later he radioed a second message to the delight of the flotilla's commanders: "Tora! Tora! Tora!" which meant "tiger," a code word indicating that the attack planes had achieved total surprise.

The expanse of Pearl Harbor unfolded below the incoming Japanese planes. One hundred thirty naval vessels, comprising the bulk of the U.S. Pacific Fleet, crowded the docks and moorings of the harbor. Among the vessels were approximately seventy warships, including eight battleships and cruisers, thirty powerful destroyers, nine minelayers, fourteen minesweepers, and four submarines. Dozens of additional support vessels— oil tankers, cargo ships, tugboats, repair ships, even a hospital ship—dotted the waters of the eight-square-mile harbor. But as the Japanese squadrons approached their targets, Fuchida saw that the harbor did not contain a single one of the aircraft carriers the fliers had hoped to destroy. This meant that one of the principal goals, the destruction of America's land air attack capability, would not be attained.

As previously arranged, Fuchida fired a blue signal flare to alert his squadrons that they had achieved total surprise. The squadron leader closest to him was to acknowledge his signal flare by rocking his plane's wings up and down. Seeing no response, Fuchida fired another flare. Confusion among the pilots soon followed. Two flares indicated that the surprise had *not* taken place. Several planes veered out of formation and flew directly to Hickam Airfield, south of the entrance to Pearl Harbor, to stop any American planes from leaving the ground. Others, including a unit of dive bombers, also misread the second flare and went to the antiaircraft guns located around the harbor. Despite this mix-up, a squadron of forty torpedo bombers remained on course and on target, gliding down to the designated altitude and heading straight for their primary objective: the battleships.

Seven blue-gray battleships were docked in two rows on the southeast side of Ford Island, in the center of Pearl Harbor. Battleship Row, as it was called, was the prime target for the Japanese. One row of five battleships—the *California, Maryland, Tennessee, Arizona*, and *Nevada*— were docked almost bow to stern along the eastern side of Ford Island. Two others—*Oklahoma* and *West Virginia*—paralleled them on the left, or port side. The vessels were in such tight formation that escape was impossible. (An eighth battleship, the *Pennsylvania*, was also present at Pearl Harbor, but it was laid up in drydock for repairs.)

Battleship Row was the primary target for the Japanese. The ripples in the water were caused by exploding torpedoes. *(Courtesy of the Naval Historical Foundation.)*

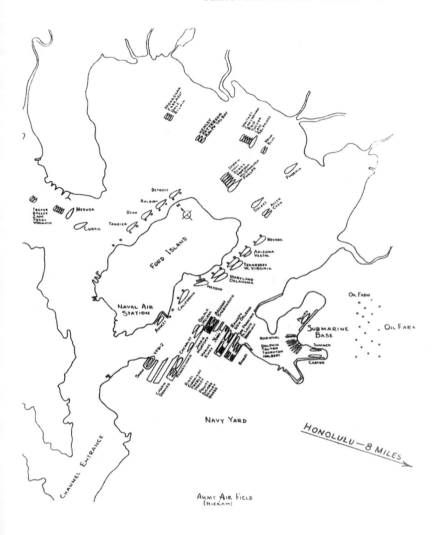

This map shows Pearl Harbor and the positions of the American ships during the attack.
(Courtesy of the Naval Historical Foundation.)

A squadron of torpedo planes from the Japanese carrier *Soryu* moved north to attack Wheeler Field, located about ten miles northwest of Pearl Harbor. Approaching the quiet field, the pilots saw to their surprise approximately 200 planes, all lined up in straight rows, wing-tip to wing-tip. The Japanese pilots laid down a line of machine gun fire. Within minutes, the attack had destroyed one out of every three planes on the ground at Wheeler Field and caused serious damage to many more. Hangars and storage buildings were also targeted. One building exploded into flames after its supply of ammunition was hit. In just a few seconds, one million rounds of machine-gun ammunition began to erupt "like an endless string of giant firecrackers."

As fighter planes prepared to launch an attack on Hickam Airfield, a dive-bomber bore down on Ford Island. The time was 7:55 a.m. As the plane pulled in low, Lieutenant Commander Logan Ramsey watched from a window in the island's command center. Angry, Ramsey phoned the station's duty officer: "Get that fellow's number," he shouted. "I want to report him for about sixteen violations!" Ramsey thought the fighter was an American "hot-dogging" over the airfield.

Seconds later, the Japanese pilot dropped a single bomb over an airplane hangar, then throttled up and out of harm's way. As the hangar exploded, the blast sent a thick cloud of black smoke into the air. Only then did Ramsey understand what he was watching. "Never mind," he informed the duty officer. "It's a Jap!"

Ramsey then dashed to the radio room, intent on

American ships and aircraft on and around Ford Island were hit by Japanese torpedoes during the attack. *(Courtesy of the Naval Historical Foundation.)*

informing as many of his fellow servicemen as possible that Pearl Harbor was under attack by Japanese air forces. At 7:58 a.m., Ramsey sent out a simple eight-word message on all frequencies in use in Hawaii: "Air raid, Pearl Harbor. This is not [a] drill." Japanese planes were soon filling the sky over the island, and, in minutes, the hangar and nearly three dozen U.S. aircraft on Ford Island were "burning like a forest fire."

Behind the dive-bomber followed a line of torpedo planes ready to hit Battleship Row. The planes came in low, their pilots concentrating on the stationary targets. As one Japanese pilot watched the assault over Pearl

Harbor, he noted that the attacking planes let loose their bombs like "dragonflies dropping their eggs."

On the deck of the battleship *Nevada*, a navy band had assembled for the 8 a.m. raising of the flags. Bandmaster Oden McMillan stood ready to strike up "The Star-Spangled Banner." Nearly all the crewmen in each of the ships surrounding Pearl Harbor were fast asleep below, taking advantage of the Sunday morning to rest. But as the band began to play the national anthem, a loud sound broke up their music. A Japanese plane swooped down on the nearby battleship *Arizona*, then pulled up and over the deck of the *Nevada*, sending naval musicians scattering. Ensign Joe Taussig, the *Nevada*'s deck officer, grabbed a microphone and shouted over the ship's public-address system: "All hands, general quarters. Air Raid!"

One of the first targeted battleships was the *Oklahoma*. Onboard, the sailors on watch were preparing to be relieved and were busy toweling the morning dew off their anti-aircraft guns. Below deck, many men slept, while the forenoon watch personnel finished their breakfast. A distant chime of church bells rang out eight o'clock. Suddenly, planes swooped near the ship. First, one torpedo struck the ship, causing a low, shattering explosion. Then, just seconds later, another pair of torpedoes found their target, ripping into the *Oklahoma*'s side, causing the vessel to take on water as she slipped to a thirty degree list. Alarms blared. Below deck, a phonograph played a popular song of the day, "Let Me Off Uptown." As the torpedoes struck the vessel, the phonograph bellowed into full volume. Soon, another torpedo slammed into the *Oklahoma*, throwing off the electricity. Emergency lights blinked on and off several times.

Minutes later, five high-level bombers attacked the wounded *Oklahoma*, each shell weighing nearly a ton. One of the bombs fell between two gun turrets on the *Oklahoma*'s deck and struck the ammunition room below. A wall of flames singed the air as these explosions caused the *Oklahoma* to shudder. As the ship began to sink, the senior officer onboard, Commander Jesse Kenworthy, ordered the crew to abandon ship. However, before they could exit, 400 crewmen and officers be-

Crewmen onboard the *USS Nevada* were taken by surprise when they were awoken by the sound of torpedo blasts on Sunday morning. This photograph shows the destruction on Battleship Row from across a farmer's field. *(Courtesy of the Naval Historical Foundation.)*

came trapped below deck with the water rising around them.

It took the Japanese only fifteen minutes to destroy the *Oklahoma*. After twenty minutes, the listing ship began to roll slowly over until her hull rose from the water and her mast lodged in the harbor's mud twenty-five feet down. The *Oklahoma* turned over so slowly that the crewmen on deck were able to walk to starboard, climb over her railing, and remain standing on her overturned hull. Some men were rescued from the overturned ship without even getting wet.

Meanwhile, another torpedo plane flew down to 100 feet, making a run at the *West Virginia*. As the pilot barked the order, his navigator-bombardier released the plane's torpedoes. Pulling up fast and making a hasty right turn, the pilot turned back to see a blast as the bombs hit the target.

In the first five minutes of the opening attack at Pearl Harbor, the Japanese fired forty torpedoes. At least half a dozen of them hit the *West Virginia*. The ship's three forward decks collapsed almost immediately. Fires broke out and engulfed the *West Virginia*'s superstructure. Power and lights across the vessel flickered and went out. Huge gaping holes in the ship's hull allowed hundreds of gallons of seawater to rush in, and soon the ship was listing thirty degrees to the port side. Crewmen thought the ship might turn completely on its side.

A unit of sailors led by Lieutenant Claude V. Ricketts, a gunnery officer on the "Wee Vee," as the *West Virginia* was called by her crew, went below to initiate counter

After being hit by at least six torpedoes, the USS *West Virginia* immediately went up in flames, causing the deaths of over 100 crewmen. *(Courtesy of the Naval Historical Foundation.)*

floods on the ship's starboard side to right her again in the water. The daring maneuver worked, and the ship was righted temporarily, but she was sinking. In just a few minutes, over 100 of the *West Virginia*'s crew were killed.

The *California*, her stern covered with a canvas awning for the morning worship services, was also soon under attack. Japanese Lieutenant Juzo Mori cut his torpedo plane across Ford Island and bore down on his battleship target. He dropped his torpedo as his plane passed only fifteen feet over the water. A heavy column of black smoke suddenly blocked his vision, and he nearly ran into a group of torpedo planes headed toward him. American forces on the ground were busy targeting Mori's plane, and machine gun bullets tore through the aircraft. His machine-gunner took a hit in the hand, and the navigator's seat cushion was struck and burst into flames. Below, the torpedo hit its mark, sending up a great explosion of water, metal, and noise. But even as the *California* began to sink and settle into the oozy cushion of mud below, sailors continued to man her anti-aircraft and machine guns.

The Japanese even targeted the dry-docked *Pennsylvania*, hitting the helpless ship with torpedoes, as well as bombing two destroyers—the *Cassin* and the *Downes*—tied up at Dry Dock No. 1. Just 300 feet away, another destroyer, the *Shaw*, sat in Floating Drydock No. 2. When hit, the *Shaw*'s forward magazine detonated, sending up a gigantic fireball of debris that reached a height of half a mile.

Everywhere throughout the eight-square-mile harbor

The USS *California* began to sink immediately after being hit by Japanese torpedoes.
(Courtesy of the Naval Historical Foundation.)

there was fire and smoke, explosions and confusion. The captain of the *West Virginia*, Mervyn Bennion, standing on his vessel's conning tower, was struck by a bomb fragment from the nearby *Tennessee* that sliced open his stomach. As he lay mortally wounded on deck, he fretted about defending his ship as fires engulfed the bridge.

The USS *Nevada* was hit first by a torpedo that ripped into the port side of her bow, causing a forty-foot-long gash in her metal hull. The ship's skipper, however, ordered the closing of the *Nevada*'s forward compartments to keep out water. Then he gave the order for the ship to get underway. As the *Nevada* began to move, she slipped past the overturned *Oklahoma*. The remaining crewmen of the *Oklahoma* cheered their comrades on as they watched the *Nevada* make a run for open water.

While many Japanese pilots targeted the battleships in Pearl Harbor, the other naval vessels were certainly not spared. At the same moment the battleships faced their first enemy torpedoes, Japanese planes flew toward a group of ships on the side of Ford Island opposite Battleship Row. At 7:55 a.m., torpedo planes from the *Hiryu* and *Soryu* dropped their loads into the shallow water, aiming for the light cruiser *Raleigh* and the target ship *Utah*. A blast struck the *Utah* and she began to flounder. Onboard the *Raleigh*, the deck officer ordered his men to take up their positions at the anti-aircraft guns. Not realizing his ship was under attack, the confused officer believed the planes were "part of a routine air-raid drill." At that moment, a torpedo hit the forward portion of *Raleigh*'s hull. All ideas of routine drills soon vanished.

Mervyn Bennion, captain of the USS *West Virginia*, died onboard his ship when a bomb fragment from the USS *Tennessee* struck him in the stomach. *(Courtesy of the Naval Historical Foundation.)*

By 8:05 a.m., the *Raleigh* was leaning to port and taking in large amounts of water.

The *Vestal*, a repair ship, and the tanker ship *Neosho* also came under attack. USS *Vestal* had just taken up its position alongside the *Arizona* the previous morning to make repairs. With a crew of 600, the officer of the deck was Ensign Fred Hall. Ironically, just the night before, in conversation with several other officers concerning possible Japanese attack targets, Hall had predicted that the Japanese would attack Pearl Harbor. As he spotted incoming Japanese planes, Hall called for general quarters at 7:55 a.m., and within ten minutes crewmen onboard the *Vestal* were firing at the enemy planes. In just minutes, two bombs struck the ship, killing a couple of sailors and wounding others.

As the battle raged, the ship caught fire. But it was the attack on the *Arizona*, docked on *Vestal*'s starboard side, that determined the fate of the repair ship. When the *Arizona* exploded, the concussion extinguished the *Vestal*'s deck fires as tons of flying metal, as well as "legs, arms and heads of men—all sorts of bodies," flew across the *Vestal*'s deck. Nearly 100 of the *Vestal*'s crew were thrown overboard, including the ship's skipper, Commander Cassin B. "Ted" Young.

The call went out to abandon ship. But just as the crew prepared to disembark, Commander Young emerged on deck, wet with oily water, shouting, "Where the hell do you think you're going?" The officer of the deck responded with a yell, "We're abandoning ship!"

Dripping and disheveled, Young thundered back his

orders: "Get back aboard ship! You don't abandon ship on me!" Some of his men hurried back to their assigned stations, while others helped the wounded out of the water.

Within an hour of the opening attack, Lieutenant Commander Samuel Fuqua of the *Arizona* ordered *Vestal*'s forward lines cut, allowing the repair ship to move away from the burning wreckage. At 8:45 a.m., *Vestal* began to draw away from Battleship Row. Damaged, she tilted to starboard. An hour later, when the Japanese attack came to an end, Commander Young ordered his vessel be run aground on a coral bed. The repair ship was in serious need of repairs herself, but she survived.

The tanker *Neosho* was docked at Berth F-4 on Ford Island near a fuel depot called the "tank farm." At its moorings, the tanker lay between the *California,* the *Tennessee,* and the *Oklahoma.* Just minutes before the Japanese attack, *Neosho* had completed a delivery of aviation gasoline to the facility. Now, in the heat of battle, there was great concern about possible gasoline explosions. If the facility or the ship exploded, it would ignite all neighboring battleships into flaming torches.

The ship's alert skipper, Captain John Phillips, prepared to move his ship away from the battleships. Within minutes, the *Neosho* was clear of Battleship Row and headed for a place of safety.

Other auxiliary ships at Pearl Harbor were not so lucky. The old minelayer *Oglala* was docked opposite Battleship Row at a berth normally reserved for the *Pennsylvania.* On *Oglala*'s port side was the cruiser *Helena.* As the bombs began to fall, Rear Admiral William Furlong, who had his quarters on the *Oglala*, watched from the ship's deck in disbelief. He thought: What a stupid, careless pilot not to have secured his releasing gear. Only after the plane cut hard to the left did Furlong see the red sun on its wings. "Japanese!" cried the admiral to the men onboard. "Man your stations!"

During the raid, one torpedo streaked through the water at the *Oglala*, slipping beneath the ship and striking the *Helena* instead. But the blast ruptured the *Oglala*'s port side hull. By 9:30 a.m., the old ship was listing about twenty degrees, causing the crew to slip and slide across her deck. Furlong ordered his men to abandon ship. Within thirty minutes the *Oglala* capsized, and, like the *Oklahoma*, "came to rest on the bottom of her port side."

Onboard the naval oil tanker *Ramapo*, located across the channel from Battleship Row, Boatswain's Mate Graff scurried down a ladder below deck where the crew lay sleeping. He yelled to his shipmates: "The Japs are bombing Pearl Harbor!" His announcement brought only blank, unbelieving stares. "No fooling," said Graff, and someone gave out a rasping Bronx cheer. Frustrated, Graff erupted: "No crap. Get your asses up on deck!"

As dozens of Japanese planes soared over the confusion, smoke, and fire of Pearl Harbor, several of the Japanese crewmen were taking photographs of the raid. Pilots wanted photos of the ships they had personally destroyed. Others wanted documentation of the attack for Japanese commanders to study after the battle.

While most of the Japanese planes concentrated on

Japanese raiders destroyed army planes at Wheeler Field.
(Courtesy of the Naval Historical Foundation.)

sea-going targets docked in Pearl Harbor, others continued to wreak havoc on the airfields around Oahu. The first airfield hit was Kaneohe Naval Air Station, located twenty miles east of Pearl Harbor. In short order, Japanese Zeros and dive-bombers destroyed all thirty-three of the station's PBY-5 (Catalina) flying boats. Aviation Ordnanceman Second Class Bert Richmond later remembered the scene: "Our planes were burning. Men were running, getting guns and ammunition, shouting and cursing."

On the ground, all was confusion. The reality of the attack was slow to sink in to the stunned American officers and enlisted men. As the Japanese began their attack on Wheeler Airfield, American personnel stood and watched, debating whether the planes were Japanese or American: "Looks like Jap planes!" one officer exclaimed. "Hell, no, it's just a Navy maneuver," another officer said.

At that moment, Brigadier General Howard C. Davidson and Colonel William Flood, Wheeler's commander, stood in shock in the doorways of their respective quarters, still wearing their pajamas. Dumbfounded, Flood wondered, "Where's our Navy? Where's our fighters?" He dropped the Sunday morning paper and rushed out to witness his base being bombed. Flood noted that he saw the enemy pilots "bombing and strafing the base, the planes, the officers' quarters, and even the golf course. I could see some of the Japanese pilots lean out of their planes and smile as they zoomed by . . . Hell, I could even see the gold in their teeth." As Davidson tried to get a clearer picture of what he was seeing, he realized his ten-year-old twin daughters were out on the family lawn, innocently picking up empty Japanese machine-gun cartridges. Terrified, he scooped them up, along with his wife, and rushed them to safety.

Few American pilots were able to take to the air to defend the bases. Most were sound asleep when the bombs began to fall. But two lieutenants did manage to reach their planes. George Welch and Ken Taylor were having breakfast in the officers' club when the Japanese divers laid down the first bombs. As the Wheeler planes were hit, Taylor and Welch commandeered a car and drove at 100 miles an hour to a small airstrip the Japanese had not targeted. They managed to get the planes into the air and fly straight into an approaching Japanese squadron. Three enemy planes were hit and crashed.

Taylor and Welch had to land and refuel before continuing their counterattack. Taking on other Japanese planes, Taylor was wounded twice that day. Welch faced the challenge of jamming machine guns onboard his plane. Taylor described one air battle: "I made a nice turn out into them and got in a string of six or eight planes. I don't know how many there were . . . I was on one's tail as we went over Waialua, firing at the one next to me, and there was one following firing at me, and I pulled out. I don't know what happened to the other plane. Lieutenant Welch, I think, shot the other man down." Indeed, Welch had saved Taylor: "We took off directly into them and shot some down. I shot down one right on Lieutenant Taylor's tail."

Before the day was over, Welch and Taylor shot down six enemy aircraft and damaged three others. Their quick action accounted for the majority of the eleven Japanese planes downed that morning by army fighter pilots. Thirty other army pilots managed to get airborne during the attack. However, not a single navy pilot hit the air. All their planes had been destroyed.

The morning of the Japanese attack, Admiral Kimmel had been up early, planning to play golf with General Short. Kimmel was on the phone discussing the submarine that had been sighted and attacked by the *Ward* when an excited commander told him that there was a message from the signal tower that the Japanese were attacking Pearl Harbor and that "this is no drill." Kimmel rushed out into his yard and witnessed the first torpedo runs.

From there, Kimmel hurried to his office, five minutes away. By his arrival the sky was full of enemy aircraft. He knew that most of his ships docked in the harbor's shallow waters were sitting ducks. He soon received a message from Rear Admiral Patrick Bellinger on Ford Island: AIR RAID, PEARL HARBOR—THIS IS NO DRILL. Kimmel sent the same message to Washington. There was little else he could do.

At Hickam Field, a 2,000-acre facility separated from Pearl Harbor by a guard fence, breakfast was being served to the soldiers when Japanese dive bombers swooped in and struck the dining hall. Silverware, metal serving trays, and glassware flew through the air like shrapnel. Most of the one hundred men in the mess hall were wounded or killed in the attack. One bomb blast killed the mess hall's entire crew of Chinese cooks who had hidden in the freezer room. One man was severely injured when struck by a shattering jar of mayonnaise.

Outside, an army chaplain had just been preparing for Sunday morning mass. Hearing the drone of airplane engines, he turned to see Japanese planes approaching. Thinking quickly, the chaplain ran to grab a machine gun resting nearby. Lacking any other available stand, the clergyman hefted the heavy .50-caliber gun and placed it on his own altar. From that unlikely perch, he began to lay down a hail of bullets at the enemy planes.

The incoming Japanese planes tore into the sixty U.S. planes grounded at Hickam, including B-17s, B-18s, and A-20s, as well as the station's facilities. As U.S. person-

Both men and equipment were lost when Japanese dive-bombers struck Hickam Field.
(Courtesy of the Naval Historical Foundation.)

nel scurried for shelter or attempted to man their guns, the Japanese pilots trained their weapons. A bomb exploded near one running soldier, killing him instantly. Later, when his buddies checked him, they only found the lower half of his uniformed body. Enemy fire cut down a master sergeant in front of the Hickam Headquarters building. Searchers later found his head severed completely from his body in a flower bed of red hibiscus. The largest of Oahu's airfields experienced a total of over 500 casualties.

In the midst of the attack at Hickam Field, the fleet of B-17s due in from California arrived, unaware of the attack. Several of the planes were caught between Japanese fighters and American artillery men, who mistook them for incoming enemy planes. The startled American pilots, attacked from the air and the ground and running perilously low on fuel, looked for safe places to land. One pilot put his B-17 down on nearby Kuhuku golf course. Miraculously, the Japanese only destroyed one of the B-17s and damaged three others.

At Schofield Barracks, north of Wheeler Field, the attack also came while soldiers were sitting down for a Sunday breakfast of pancakes and two pints of milk each. The men heard the explosions at Pearl Harbor before an enemy plane roared over the army facility, strafing the ground and buildings with .50-caliber machine gun fire. The men dove for cover, hiding behind any protection they could find. Two angry soldiers, Sergeant Lowell Klatt and Lieutenant Stephen Saltzman, returned fire as well as they could, futilely emptying their Browning Automatic Rifles at the incoming dive-bombers. Those with cool heads manned the various machine gun emplacements around the barracks and returned fire on the enemy.

James Jones, an army private, was among those at breakfast as the enemy swooped in. (Jones would later write a popular novel about life in the pre-war Schofield Barracks entitled *From Here to Eternity*.) As the young soldier stood outside the mess hall with his comrades, he watched as a Zero brandishing the stark red sun of Imperial Japan streaked over an asphalt camp road, its machine guns blazing in two rows along the road. As the Zero passed Private Jones, he clearly saw the pilot, who wore a white headband over his helmet. The silk band, or *hachimaki*, was decorated with a red sun that covered the Japanese pilot's forehead. In writing about the incident, Jones recalled that the pilot had smiled and waved at him.

Chapter Six

The Second Wave

The second wave of 170 Japanese planes arrived at Pearl Harbor at 8:55 a.m. It included fifty-four bombers that headed back to Hickam Field and the Naval Air Station at Kaneohe, and eighty dive-bombers whose target was the U.S. Fleet, already crippled in the harbor. Another thirty-six Zeros joined in the fray.

By now the U.S. resistance was better organized, and Japanese losses increased. American anti-aircraft fire downed twenty-one planes. Also, the second wave of dive-bombers were hampered in their efforts by the clouds of thick, black smoke rising over their targets.

Nearly every large ship in the harbor was on fire by the time the second wave of enemy planes arrived. The *Oklahoma* had flipped over completely. The *California* was sunk, resting in the harbor mud. Oily fires engulfed the wreckage of the *Arizona,* and the *West Virginia*, already on fire, was sinking. Putting out the fires was almost impossible. The fire brigade on Ford Island was confounded by a lack of water pressure. When the *Ari-*

zona sank, it had settled on the island's primary water pipes.

Only two of the seven gray vessels lined up on Battleship Row survived the day with minimal damage. Because the *Maryland* and the *Tennessee* were docked on the starboard side of the *Oklahoma* and the *West Virginia*, they were protected from Japanese torpedoes. The *Maryland* was only hit by one bomb from Fuchida's squadrons. The *Tennessee* sustained a couple of bomb hits but ended up with light damage.

Several Japanese planes now prepared to attack a moving target, the battleship *Nevada,* which still pushed to escape the harbor. Dive bombers filled the sky above the fleeing vessel when a barrage of anti-aircraft fire poured into the sky. Two enemy planes spiraled into the harbor. The smoke raised by the firing from the ship's guns completely cloaked her for a time.

As the *Nevada* raced out beyond Battleship Row, fires streaked across the deck. A Japanese bomb had torn into a starboard gun battery. Another bomb shattered through the deck. But the *Nevada* pushed on amidst the smoke and fire.

It was clear to U.S. officials that the *Nevada*'s movement into the channel might threaten the remainder of the fleet at Pearl Harbor. If the ship were sunk in the narrow channel, no other vessel would be able to escape. Hurriedly, signal corpsmen scrambled up on the naval district water tower to signal the desperate order to the *Nevada* to remain clear of the channel.

With no place else to go, the officers onboard ordered

the ship to move toward shore. A pair of navy tugboats moved in to assist. The ship finally ran aground at Waipio Point, with the channel just ahead. Two, four, five, then six more bombs pounded the *Nevada* and her crew before it stopped. Crewmen battled the ship's intense fires. Although the ship's superstructure—masts, guns, towers—was severely damaged, the ship was saved. Fifty members of her crew had been killed, including three officers, and twice as many were wounded.

The crewmen stranded on the exposed hull of the *Oklahoma* were facing their own private hell. Even with the ship overturned and completely destroyed, Japanese planes continued to bomb her. Zero pilots wheeled above and headed straight for the ship's survivors, strafing the sailors with machine gun fire.

The USS *Arizona* at sea during the 1930s, before the attack at Pearl Harbor.
(Courtesy of the Naval Historical Foundation.)

During the first wave of attack, the USS *Arizona*, a battleship dating back to World War I, had been missed by the torpedo planes. But now, high-level bombers struck the vessel with five direct hits. One of the bombs dropped through the forecastle, igniting the ship's fuel-storage compartment below deck. A fire erupted and an explosion heaved the ship open. The fire had detonated 1,600 pounds of highly-combustible black powder stored on the *Arizona* against naval regulations. This gigantic explosion detonated hundreds of tons of smokeless powder also stored onboard in the ship's forward powder magazines that held 300 fourteen-inch shells, 3,500 five-inch shells, and at least 100,000 rounds of machine-gun ammo. In all, the belly of the *Arizona* was filled with nearly two million pounds of explosives.

Filled with two million pounds of explosives, The USS *Arizona* (center) split in two when it was bombed. *(Courtesy of the Naval Historical Foundation.)*

The *Arizona* nearly rose out of the water, the upward thrust splitting the ship in two. Flames engulfed the twisted wreckage as the *Arizona* sank, embroiled in acrid, black smoke from a wall of oil-fed flame forming on the ship's halves. The explosion was so intense that its concussion rocked Commander Fuchida's plane flying two miles above. Fuchida himself later described what he saw: "It was a hateful, mean-looking, red flame, the kind that powder produces. I knew a big powder magazine had exploded." Onboard the *Arizona*, nearly 1,500 men went down. All along Battleship Row men were trying to swim from burning ships, but after the *Arizona* exploded, the harbor surface was coated with oil that burst into flames. Deck fires blazed so fiercely that crewmen on the nearby *Nevada* had to lay themselves down as shields to cover their artillery shells to keep them from exploding. Debris from the *Arizona* accounted for most of damage to the *Tennessee*, which was positioned on the *Arizona*'s starboard.

The explosion killed Rear Admiral Isaac Kidd and the ship's captain, Franklin Van Valkenburgh, who were positioned on the *Arizona*'s flag bridge. The blast was so intense that no part of Admiral Kidd was ever recovered, with the exception of his gold naval academy class ring, found melded into the ship's steel conning tower.

The Japanese had not targeted Honolulu because it was not considered an important military objective. Stunned civilians watched and listened to the events that morning at Pearl Harbor and the other bases. Some refused to believe that the planes, explosions, and col-

The USS *Arizona* became engulfed in thick flames and smoke as it began to sink.
(Courtesy of the Naval Historical Foundation.)

umns of black smoke were not all part of an elaborate military exercise. Little of downtown Honolulu was damaged. In fact, falling shrapnel from American anti-aircraft guns did more damage to the city than Japanese bombs.

American sailors worked to rescue their comrades trapped in sinking and burning ships. Onboard the *West Virginia*, oily water seeped in and threatened to engulf the trapped crewmen. Ensign Victor Delano and several other sailors moved quickly ahead of the rising water, slipping repeatedly on the oil-slicked passageway. Struggling to make their way out of the ship, they could hear the cries of sailors trapped behind closed doors. The ship's damage-control officer had ordered the watertight doors shut to slow down the ship's sinking, but the men locked inside almost faced certain drowning. Some escaped through portholes, and others, such as Ensign Delano, worked their way to the upper decks to safety.

Men onboard the *Oklahoma* also faced great danger. Hundreds of men were trapped onboard the upside-down ship. Their world was now a topsy-turvy nightmare of water, darkness, and terror. Many of the watertight compartments of the floundered ship still contained air, allowing the men to breath. But everyone understood the air would not last. Men frantically banged on the metal walls and pipes of their compartments to let rescuers know where they were.

About thirty of the *Oklahoma*'s crew were trapped in the ship's dispensary. After waiting an hour for rescue, they took their own initiative. To remain in the dispen-

Soldiers were not the only ones in danger during the attack on Pearl Harbor. These three civilians were killed as they drove in their car. *(Courtesy of the Naval Historical Foundation.)*

sary would mean certain death by suffocation. As men dove down into the room's oily water, they discovered a porthole. Although uncertain where it led, they took their chances. As luck would have it, swimming through the porthole brought many of the men to the surface. Sadly, however, some were too large to squeeze through the porthole to safety. For them, the dispensary became their tomb.

When one group of sailors on the *Oklahoma* was trapped in the center portion of the ship, all seemed lost. There appeared to be no way out. Then one of the men dove into the water that filled the decks of the capsized ship. He swam until he found the ship's submerged deck, and back up again to the surface. He then led a rescue operation to save his shipmates.

Another group of thirty survivors found an air pocket three decks down inside the *Oklahoma*. All the sailors could do was strike on the metal walls to indicate their location. But no one came. Seaman Stephen Young prayed: "God, please get us out of this." As the hours ticked by, man after man attempted to swim to safety through the darkened passageways of their upside-down ship. But none made it. After twenty-five hours inside the ship, Young and nine others were finally rescued when their comrades broke into the chamber using pneumatic hammers.

Rescuers faced two main problems. First, they attempted to locate trapped crewmen by listening for their knocking on the metal walls of the ship, but pinpointing exactly where such sounds came from was difficult. Sometimes rescuers cut into a portion of the ship's hull but found no one inside. The second problem was the nature of the tools of rescue. When acetylene torches were used to cut through metal, the torches consumed the air in the chamber, suffocating the trapped men. Pneumatic drills broke into airtight chambers, letting the air escape, which in turn caused the water to rise, thus drowning the trapped sailors in the compartment.

The rescued and the wounded needed immediate medical treatment and, soon after the attack, the Pearl Harbor Naval Hospital reached its capacity of patients. Some wounded—many bearing serious burns from the explosions and oil fires—were sent to additional base hospitals, such as the Fort Shafter facility, and to civilian hospitals in Honolulu. Surgeons amputated many limbs that were damaged beyond repair. Dr. John Cooper, operating at Tripler General Hospital, remembered, "there were legs and arms in twenty-five to forty large GI galvanized cans, waiting for disposal."

Chapter Seven

Infamy

The surprise attack on the American installations on Oahu took two hours. The second wave of attackers began to withdraw at 9:50 a.m. Just two hours after that, all the Japanese planes that had survived the raid were back safe onboard their home ships. No sooner had the successful planes landed, then Commander Fuchida spoke in favor of a third attack. But Admiral Nagumo refused. He believed that the pilots of the Strike Force had succeeded in their efforts to destroy the U.S. Pacific Fleet.

In just two hours, Japanese planes had destroyed or seriously damaged eighteen American war vessels, including all eight battleships. At least 160 American planes were damaged beyond repair, and an equal number were damaged. By comparison, the Japanese lost five midget submarines and twenty-nine planes.

The real losses of the day, however, were human lives. About 2,500 Americans were killed, including more than 2,400 U.S. sailors, soldiers, pilots, and Marines. Another 1,200 were wounded. The invaders only counted their dead at sixty-four. A midget sub's captain was the only captive taken by Americans.

However, despite the apparent success of the Japanese attack, some fundamental mistakes had been made. The raiding pilots had been ordered to destroy planes and ships. As a result, they did not target the huge storage tanks located at Pearl Harbor, filled with millions of barrels of oil. The navy shipyard was still largely intact and set to work immediately to repair the damaged ships. Most of the naval ammunition stores escaped, and dozens of smaller war vessels had not been hit. Lastly, the most instrumental vessels of the American fleet, the aircraft carriers, were not docked at Pearl Harbor that morning. They, along with many of the ships that survived the Pearl Harbor attack, including some of the battleships, could now spearhead the American war effort in the Pacific against the Japanese.

As word of the invasion reached the Japanese public, the civilian population was ecstatic. They believed their military had carried out a great and honorable victory. In America, news of the attack infuriated the entire population. While most people in America had opposed U.S. involvement in the ever-expanding war in Asia, they were now prepared to fight a war of revenge against Imperial Japan. Politicians who had led the fight against U.S. involvement in World War II now made press announcements that the time for debate was over and it was time to go to war.

That afternoon, in Washington, D.C., Secretary of State Cordell Hull met for the last time with Japanese

President Franklin D. Roosevelt petitioned Congress on December 8, 1941, to declare war on Japan. *(Courtesy of the Naval Historical Foundation.)*

diplomats. He was handed a message at 2:20 p.m., after the attack at Pearl Harbor was over. The message did not even acknowledge the strike. It only accused the United States of refusing to negotiate in good faith. Hull, after months of fruitless diplomacy, lost his patience. He had known the Japanese were planning a military move. He spoke harshly with the two Japanese diplomats and dismissed them stiffly. As they exited his office for the last time, an exasperated Hull muttered, "Scoundrels and pissants!"

Admiral Yamamoto received word from Strike Force officers that the attack against Pearl Harbor had been carried out successfully. He was disappointed when he discovered that the attack had taken place before Japanese diplomats had delivered an official declaration of war to U.S. leaders. "I fear that we have awakened a sleeping giant and filled him with a terrible resolve," he commented to an aide. Shortly thereafter, Yamamoto wrote a letter to his sister, expressing his concerns about the meaning of the Pearl Harbor attack: "The sinking of four or five battleships is no cause for celebration. There will be times of defeat as well as victory."

The day after the attack, December 8, 1941, President Franklin D. Roosevelt appeared before a joint session of Congress. Beginning his speech with a phrase that is now famous: "Yesterday, December 7—a date that will live in infamy—the United States of America was sud-

Franklin Delano Roosevelt signed a declaration of war against Japan after the bombing on Pearl Harbor. *(Courtesy of the Library of Congress.)*

denly and deliberately attacked . . ." he asked Congress for a declaration of war against Japan. His words were met with a standing ovation and Congress took only an hour to approve the request. Because Japan had signed an agreement with Germany and Italy, those two European nations soon declared war on the U.S. For the first time, the United States was engaged in war in Asia and Europe simultaneously.

By August 1942, Japan had conquered most of Southeast Asia, including Indonesia and the Philippines. For the remainder of the war in the Pacific, the Allied nations would fight to remove Japanese troops from these areas. It was not until August 1945, when President Franklin D. Roosevelt ordered the atomic bombing of the Japanese cities of Nagasaki and Hiroshima, that Japan was again reduced to its original size.

The success of the attack on Pearl Harbor remains debatable. While the sinking of twenty-one ships did slow America's ability to react to Japanese strikes elsewhere in the Pacific, it did little to ensure long term success. Most of the ships destroyed were old—the *Arizona* had been launched in 1915—and their removal made way for the building of a new class of ship. One U.S. admiral even remarked that the Japanese "did us a favor [by] destroying a lot of old hardware."

More importantly, the destruction of the U.S. battleships ushered in a new era for naval warfare. The loss of its battleships forced the U.S. Navy to reconfigure itself around the aircraft carriers that remained. Like the Japanese strategy to attack Pearl Harbor, from now on, the

Doris Miller, a mess hall attendant aboard the USS *West Virginia*, received the Navy Cross for shooting down Japanese fighter planes. *(Courtesy of the Naval Historical Foundation.)*

navy would center its plans for battle around aircraft carriers that transported planes to engage in air attacks. This new strategy replaced the one-on-one fights between battleships of the past and dramatically increased the importance of aircraft carriers. For instance, when four Japanese carriers were sunk in the Battle of Midway, which lasted from June 4-7, 1942, the Japanese suffered a more decisive defeat than America had suffered at Pearl Harbor.

That the attack on Pearl Harbor was a propaganda victory for the United States is certainly clear. The resulting anger that swept over America fueled the build-up of the most massive war machine ever seen. In a matter of weeks the nation's factories had been converted for wartime production. Millions of men and women had been called to service, and political leaders were determined to win the war in both Europe and the Pacific. Winston Churchill, the Prime Minister of Great Britain, later remarked that the United States was like a great pot of water that was slow to boil, but once it got going "there was no limit to the power it could generate."

The deaths of approximately 2,500 Americans on December 7, 1941, (more than half of which were lost when the *Arizona* exploded) marked the entrance of the United States into one of the worst wars in human history. As a result, the United States was forced to rebuild its navy, instigate new military strategies, and halt domestic industry to focus instead on military expansion. These measures would not only help to ensure the Allied victory, but would also lead to the introduction of the

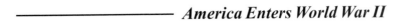

atomic bomb, making the attack on Pearl Harbor one of the most critical events of the twentieth century.

Timeline

1931—Japanese forces occupy the Chinese province of Manchuria.

1936—Japanese military controls the civilian government.

1937—President Roosevelt publicly protests Japan's actions against China and condemns Japanese aggression.

1938—President Roosevelt receives funding from Congress for "two-ocean" U.S. Navy.

1939—Roosevelt orders U.S. Pacific Naval Fleet from San Diego to new headquarters in Hawaii at Pearl Harbor.

1940—July: Roosevelt orders restrictions on shipments of American scrap metal, lubricating oil, and aviation fuel to the Japanese.

August: U.S. cryptologists break Japanese diplomatic code. Codename: "Operation Magic."

September 27: Japanese officially ally themselves with Germany and Italy.

1941—January: Admiral Yamamoto begins plans for
  Japanese attack at Pearl Harbor.
  February: Japanese Naval Commander Minoru
  Genda fine tunes Yamamoto's proposed invasion
  plans.
  Summer: Japanese pilots train in city of
  Kagoshima to prepare for Pearl Harbor attack.
  July: Japanese invasion and occupation of French
  Indochina.
  July 26: FDR freezes Japanese credit in the U.S.
  October 18: Tojo replaces Prince Konoye as Prime
  Minister, establishing hardline, military leader-
  ship.
  November 5: Magic intercepts six Japanese diplo-
  matic messages ordering the completion of
  negotiations with the U.S. by November 25.
  November 16: U.S. Navy Intelligence loses track of
  Japanese carriers that comprise Strike Force.
  November 20: Japanese offer to withdraw from
  Indochina in exchange for end of U.S. oil embargo.
  November 21: Japan postpones deadline for
  negotiations until November 29.
  November 26: Admiral Nagumo's First Air Fleet
  leaves the Kurile Isles with his Strike Force bound
  for Hawaii. Secretary of State Hull counters
  Japanese diplomatic proposal with insistence that
  Japan must withdraw from both Indochina and
  China.
  November 27: U.S. General Short orders precautions

against Japanese saboteurs at American airfields in Hawaii.

November 29: Imperial meeting accepts inevitability of war with United States.

December 2: Yamamoto sends "Climb Mount Niitaka" message in code to Strike Fleet.

December 5: Last U.S. aircraft carrier still at Pearl Harbor, *Lexington*, leaves Hawaii for Midway.

December 7:

6:30 a.m.—First wave of Japanese Strike Force takes off from aircraft carriers bound for Pearl Harbor. American vessel spots Japanese midget submarine attempting to enter Pearl Harbor.

7:00 a.m.—USS *Ward* sinks Japanese midget sub.

7:02 a.m.—Radar station personnel Lockhard and Elliott sight Japanese planes 130 miles out from Hawaii.

7:20 a.m.—Lt. Tyler "identifies" radar blip as U.S. B-17s due in from California.

7:25 a.m.—Admiral Kimmel informed of Ward's sinking of Japanese sub.

7:49 a.m.—Fuchida radios "To, To, To" message in code, meaning "charge."

7:53 a.m.—Fuchida radios "Tora, Tora, Tora" message, meaning "tiger," indicating the Japanese had achieved surprise against the Americans.

7:55 a.m.—First wave of Japanese planes begins attack against Oahu installations.

9:00 a.m.—Second wave of Japanese planes begins attack.

By 9:45 a.m.—Japanese attack is completed, resulting in the

sinking of eighteen ships, destroying or damaging nearly 350 U.S. planes, and killing nearly 2,500 U.S. military personnel.

December 8—President Roosevelt requests a declaration of war from Congress against Japan.

Bibliography

Barker, Arthur J. *Pearl Harbor*. New York: Ballantine
    Books, 1969.

Barnes, Harry. E. *Pearl Harbor After a Quarter of a Century*.
    New York: Arno Press, 1972.

Bonaventura, Ray, and Ralph Vecchi. *Month of Infamy,
    December 1941*. Culver City, CA: Venture
    Publications, 1976.

Clark, Blake. *Remember Pearl Harbor!* New York: Modern
    Age Books, 1942.

Costello, John. *The Pacific War 1941-1945*. New York:
    Rawson and Wade, 1981.

Dallek, Robert. *Franklin D. Roosevelt and American Foreign
    Policy, 1932-1945*. New York: Oxford University
    Press, 1979.

Feis, Herbert. *The Road to Pearl Harbor: The Coming of War Between the United States and Japan*. Princeton: Princetown University Press, 1950.

Heiferman, Ronald. *US Navy in World War II*. London: Bison Books, 1978.

Hoehling. A. A. *The Week Before Pearl Harbor*. New York: W. W. Norton, 1963.

Kahn, David. *The Codebreakers*. New York: Alfred A. Knopf, 1946.

Langer, William L. and S. Everett Gleason. *The Undeclared War: 1940-1941*. New York: Harper & Brothers, 1953.

Lord, Walter. *Day of Infamy*. New York: Henry Holt and Company, 1957.

Mitchell, Joseph B and Sir Edward Creasy. *Twenty Decisive Battles of the World*. New York: Macmillan, 1964.

Parkinson, Roger. *Attack at Pearl Harbor*. London: Wayland, 1973.

Prange, Gordon W. December 7, 1941: *The Day the Japanese Attacked Pearl Harbor*. New York: McGraw-Hill, 1988.

———. *At Dawn We Slept*. New York: McGraw-Hill, 1981.

Shapiro, William E. *Pearl Harbor*. New York: Franklin Watts, 1984.

Stillwell, Paul, ed. *Air Raid: Pearl Harbor!* Annapolis, MD: U.S. Naval Institute Press, 1981.

Toland, John. *But Not in Shame*. New York: Random House, 1961.

———. *The Rising Sun*. New York: Random House, 1970.

———. Infamy: *Pearl Harbor and Its Aftermath*. Garden City, NY: Doubleday, 1982.

Van de Vat, Dan. *The Pacific Campaign, World War II: The US and Japanese Naval War, 1941-1945*. New York: Simon and Schuster, 1991.

Zich, Arthur. *The Rising Sun*. Alexandria, Virginia: Time-Life Books., 1977.

Websites

Pearl Harbor Remembered
www.execpc.com/~dschaaf/mainmenu.html

USS *Arizona* Memorial (National Park Service)
www.nps.gov/usar/

Pearl Harbor Attacked
www.pearlharborattacked.com

Index

Russo-Japanese War of 1925, 28, 32, 44

Saltzman, Stephen, 82
Shaw, 70
Shokaku, 44-45
Short, Walter C., 41-42, 54, 79
Soryu, 44-45
Stark, Harold R., 41

Taussig, Joe, 66
Taylor, Ken, 78-79
Tennessee, 52, 62, 72, 75, 85, 88
Togo, Shigenori, 53
Tojo, Hideki, 22, 30, 50
Tri-Partite Pact, 23-24, 28, 30

Utah, 72

Van Valkenburg, Franklin, 88
Vestal, 74-75

Ward, 10-11, 58
Welch, George, 78-79
West Virginia, 52, 62, 68, *69*, 70-72, 84-85, 90
World War I, 12, 17

Yamamoto, Isoroku, 25-26, *27*, 28, 31-37, 50, 96-97

Yamashita, Tomoyuki, 24-25, 30
Yosuke, Matsuoka, 17, *18*, 22-23
Young, Cassin B. "Ted," 74-75
Young, Stephen, 92

Zuikaku, 44-45